weird but true!

DISNEY

NATIONAL GEOGRAPHIC KiDS

weird but true!

DISNEY

300 WONDERFUL FACTS TO CELEBRATE THE MAGIC OF DISNEY

NATIONAL GEOGRAPHIC
WASHINGTON, D.C.

When ride vehicles from **Dumbo the Flying Elephant** and the **Mad Tea Party** were donated to the Smithsonian Institution, they received a **police escort** through **Washington, D.C.**

5

SPACESHIP EARTH at EPCOT weighs about 16 million pounds (7 million kg).

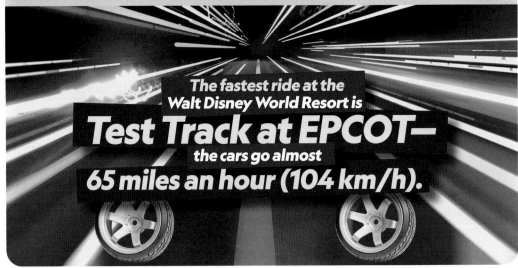

The fastest ride at the Walt Disney World Resort is **Test Track at EPCOT—** *the cars go almost* **65 miles an hour (104 km/h).**

On **SPACE MOUNTAIN** at the Magic Kingdom, a spaceship's signage reads H-NCH 1975, which refers to the last name of the ride's designer (Hench) and the year the ride opened.

To honor Walt Disney today, a lamp in the window is always lit.

Walt Disney had an apartment above the Town Square Fire Station at Disneyland.

The actor who voiced Donald Duck also voiced the dog barks for **One Hundred and One Dalmatians (1961).**

Cucumbers in The Land pavilion greenhouses at EPCOT are grown in the shape of **Mickey Mouse's head.**

The **water** in the **Jungle Cruise** attraction is **dyed.**

THIRTEEN LANTERNS hang from the Liberty Tree in **Liberty Square** at the Magic Kingdom—each represents one of America's original **13 Colonies.**

ROCK 'N' ROLLER COASTER

STARRING AEROSMITH

AT DISNEY'S HOLLYWOOD STUDIOS LAUNCHES RIDERS AT A SPEED OF 60 MILES AN HOUR (96 km/h) IN 2.8 SECONDS.

Animators studied the movement of Rapunzel's hair in *Tangled* (2010) **to create the movement of the ocean** in *Moana* (2016).

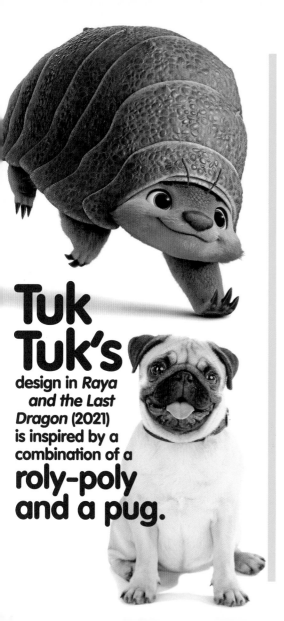

Tuk Tuk's design in *Raya and the Last Dragon* (2021) is inspired by a combination of a **roly-poly and a pug.**

THE REPLICA OF THE LIBERTY BELL

IN LIBERTY SQUARE AT THE MAGIC KINGDOM WAS BUILT FROM THE **SAME CAST AS THE ORIGINAL.**

THE
**ANIMAL
CARE
TEAM**
AT DISNEY'S
ANIMAL KINGDOM
PREPARES
MORE THAN
**4.5 TONS
(4 T)
OF FOOD
A DAY.**

WALT DISNEY was the voice of **MICKEY MOUSE** for almost 20 years.

One dress worn in *Descendants 2* (2017) took more than **100 yards** (91 m) **of fabric** to make—that's almost the height of the Statue of Liberty.

The director of *Lightyear (2022)* **built LEGO®️ models** to share ideas for **BUZZ'S SPACESHIP** with fellow filmmakers.

A MAGIC TRICK from the 1800s makes **dancing ghosts** appear in the ballroom of the **Haunted Mansion** attraction.

The animated dogs in **One Hundred and One Dalmatians** (1961) sport a total of 6,469,952 spots.

THE ARTISTS WHO DESIGN AND CREATE EACH DETAIL OF **DISNEY** THEME PARKS **ARE CALLED IMAGINEERS—** A COMBINATION OF **"IMAGINATION"** AND **"ENGINEER."**

A sign on **Test Track** at **EPCOT** shows the number **82,** which references **the year** the theme park opened.

CRATERS ON THE PLANET MERCURY FORM THE SHAPE OF **MICKEY MOUSE'S HEAD.**

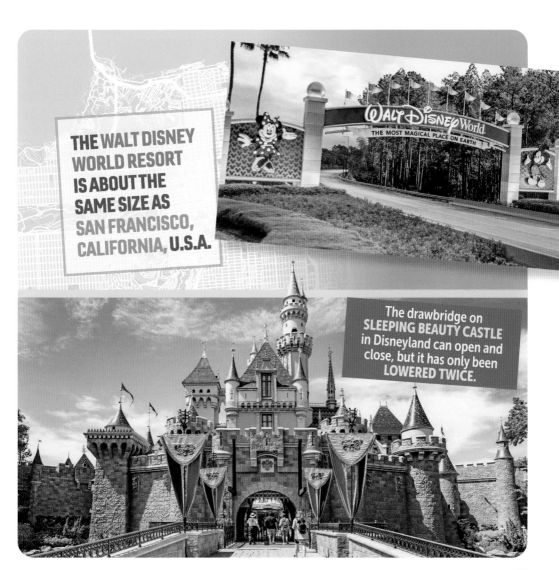

THE WALT DISNEY WORLD RESORT IS ABOUT THE SAME SIZE AS SAN FRANCISCO, CALIFORNIA, U.S.A.

The drawbridge on **SLEEPING BEAUTY CASTLE** in Disneyland can open and close, but it has only been **LOWERED TWICE.**

Filming **STOPPED** on *Swiss Family Robinson* (1960) when **100 FLAMINGO "STARS"** suddenly migrated **SOUTH.**

The first words Mickey Mouse spoke were "Hot dog!" in a 1929 cartoon.

The **NAMES ON THE TOMBSTONES** outside the Haunted Mansion in the Magic Kingdom and Disneyland represent the Imagineers who created the attraction.

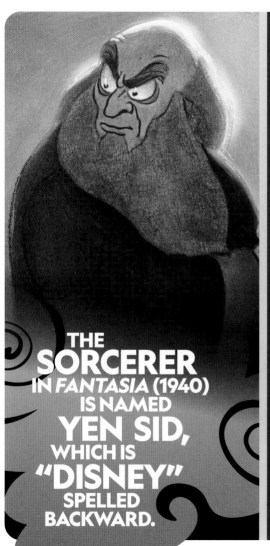

THE SORCERER IN *FANTASIA* (1940) IS NAMED **YEN SID,** WHICH IS **"DISNEY"** SPELLED BACKWARD.

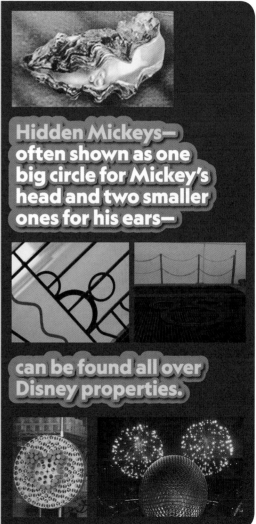

Hidden Mickeys— often shown as one big circle for Mickey's head and two smaller ones for his ears— can be found all over Disney properties.

TWO SOLAR FACILITIES AT WALT DISNEY WORLD RESORT PROVIDE ENOUGH RENEWABLE ENERGY ANNUALLY TO OPERATE TWO OF THE RESORT'S FOUR THEME PARKS.

ONE FACILITY IS IN THE SHAPE OF MICKEY MOUSE'S HEAD.

Animators **HANDCRAFTED** hundreds of thousands of **BUBBLES** for *The Little Mermaid* (1989).

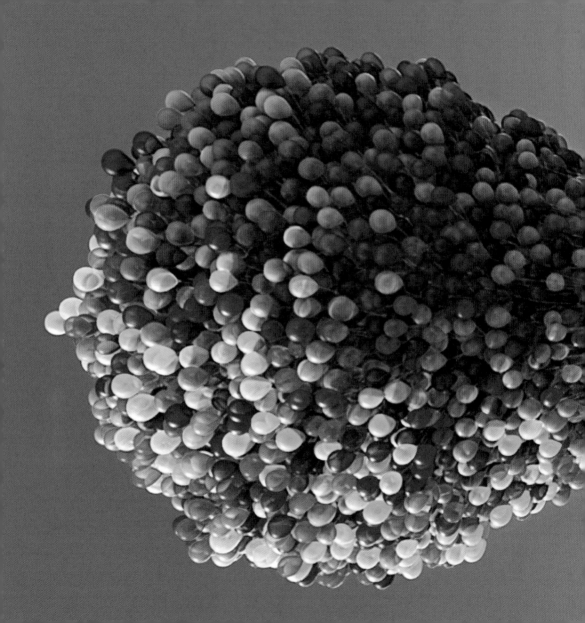

In *Up* (2009), 20,622 balloons lifted Carl's house, but it would take more than 20 million balloons to carry it in real life.

Walt Disney originally wanted to name Mickey Mouse **"MORTIMER."**

Toy blocks in the nursery in Peter Pan's Flight in Disneyland spell "Peter Pan."

A **special machine** blasts specific scents in different park attractions, such as salty sea air in Pirates of the Caribbean.

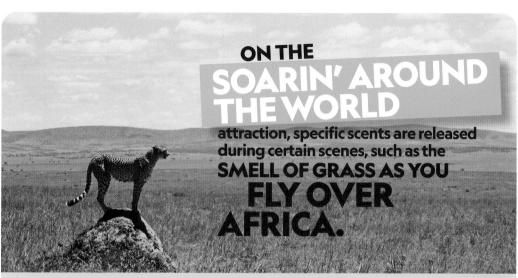

ON THE
SOARIN' AROUND THE WORLD

attraction, specific scents are released during certain scenes, such as the **SMELL OF GRASS AS YOU FLY OVER AFRICA.**

It took animators MORE THAN TWO YEARS to create the two-and-a-half-minute wildebeest stampede in *The Lion King* (1994).

Dumbo is the only title character from a Disney animated feature film who never speaks.

WHEN ALADDIN LIES TO JASMINE ABOUT BEING A PRINCE, THE FEATHER ON HIS HAT FALLS IN HIS FACE.

Snow White is the only Disney Princess with a star on the Hollywood Walk of Fame.

SNOW WHITE

Rapunzel's hair in *Tangled* (2010) has about 140,000 strands.

Walt Disney's **first named animated character** —was— **Julius the cat.**

Astronomers researched what the night skies would have

SCIENTISTS FROM
DISNEY'S ANIMAL KINGDOM
DISCOVERED THAT
elephants make
a specific call
to warn their herd that
bees are nearby.

looked like 2,000 years ago for **Moana** (2016).

Artists used more than
800 gallons
**(3,028 L) of paint
to animate**
*One Hundred and
One Dalmatians* **(1961)—
that's enough
to cover about**
15 football
fields.

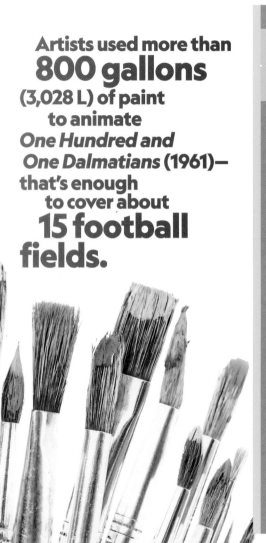

A SERIES OF TUNNELS
CALLED THE UTILIDOR
WAS BUILT UNDERNEATH
THE MAGIC KINGDOM
AT WALT DISNEY WORLD.

CAST MEMBERS USE
THESE TUNNELS TO GET TO
THEIR WORK LOCATIONS—
WALT DISNEY WANTED
IT TO SEEM AS IF THEY
APPEAR BY MAGIC.

Goofy's original name was Dippy Dawg.

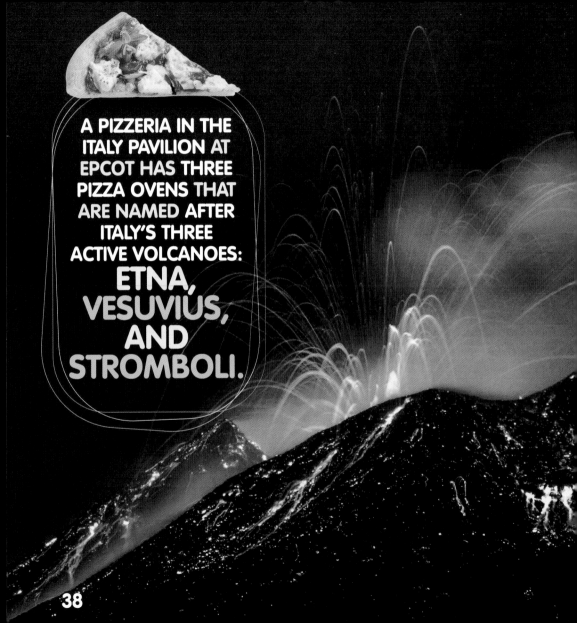

A PIZZERIA IN THE ITALY PAVILION AT EPCOT HAS THREE PIZZA OVENS THAT ARE NAMED AFTER ITALY'S THREE ACTIVE VOLCANOES: **ETNA, VESUVIUS, AND STROMBOLI.**

Part of the live-action *Mulan* (2020) was filmed in China's Mingsha Mountains, which make a musical sound when the wind blows across them.

Main Street, U.S.A. in Disneyland draws inspiration from Walt Disney's hometown of Marceline, Missouri.

A restaurant in
Cinderella Castle
in the Magic Kingdom once offered diners medieval costumes to wear.

THE
WALT DISNEY WORLD RAILROAD
IN THE MAGIC KINGDOM OPERATES FOUR STEAM-POWERED TRAINS, SOME OF WHICH ARE
MORE THAN 100 YEARS OLD.

On **Main Street, U.S.A.** at Disney parks, names of people who were important to each park appear on the windows.

There's a basketball hoop **inside** the Matterhorn mountain in Disneyland.

There is **no** **electric light** in *Encanto* (2021)— every scene is lit with candles, the sun, the moon, **or magic.**

Mirabel's name is inspired by the Spanish word ***mira***, meaning "look," which reflects the movie's theme of seeing people for **who they truly are.**

43

There's a suite inside Cinderella Castle in the Magic Kingdom.

On the **KILIMANJARO SAFARIS** savanna at Disney's Animal Kingdom, air is piped into rocks to **cool the cats.**

MORE THAN 4,000 PAIRS OF EARS were sculpted for the LEPrecon characters in *Artemis Fowl* (2020).

AT DISNEY'S ANIMAL KINGDOM, THE **TREE OF LIFE** HAS MORE THAN **300** ANIMAL IMAGES CARVED INTO ITS TRUNK AND ROOTS.

The animated Beast in *Beauty and the Beast* (1991) is inspired by a mix of a lion, a buffalo, a wild boar, a gorilla, a wolf, and a bear.

Vegetables grown in The Land pavilion at **EPCOT** are used in some of the park's restaurants.

When rain falls on **Spaceship Earth** at EPCOT, the water is funneled through the sphere and into the park's **World Showcase Lagoon.**

The 29 GOLD SPHERES on the moon model in Mission: Space at Planetary Plaza at EPCOT represent the 29 U.S. and Soviet Union lunar landing missions between 1959 and 1976.

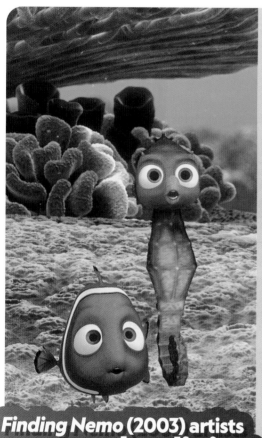

Finding Nemo (2003) artists went **scuba diving** to ensure the animated characters' **accuracy.**

It took **28 people to operate** the remote controls that moved the mechanical **giant squid** in *20,000 Leagues Under the Sea* (1954).

The rooms in Disney's Contemporary Resort, near the Magic Kingdom, were built elsewhere, and then cranes slid them into the building's framework.

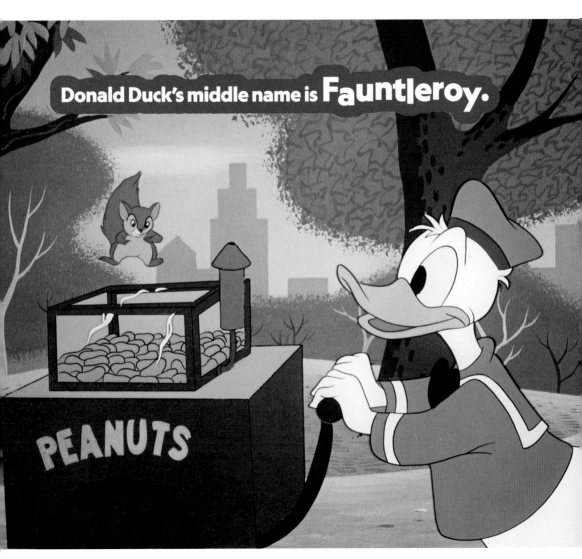

Donald Duck's middle name is **Fauntleroy.**

TO CELEBRATE ITS

25th ANNIVERSARY,

THE WALT DISNEY WORLD RESORT
TRANSFORMED

Cinderella Castle

INTO A CAKE, USING

400 gallons (1,514 L)

OF **PINK** PAINT.

It was topped with candles as high as 40 feet (12 m), 30 three-foot (0.9-m)-wide **lollipops,** and four 25-foot (7.6-m) stacks of **ring-shaped candies.**

51

SOME OF WALT DISNEY'S INSPIRATION FOR DISNEYLAND CAME FROM WATCHING HIS DAUGHTERS RIDE A MERRY-GO-ROUND.

One of Walt Disney's inspirations for **Sleeping Beauty Castle** in Disneyland was Neuschwanstein Castle in Germany.

In the line for Slinky Dog Dash in Toy Story Land at Disney's Hollywood Studios, a Rex toy box shows a **$19.95 price tag,** which refers to the year that *Toy Story* opened in theaters.

TYRANNOSAURUS REX
- Tyrannosaurus means "Tyrant Lizard" in Ancient Greek, and Rex means "King" in Latin
- The most feared dinosaur of the Cretaceous Period
- One of the largest carnivorous dinosaurs with an enormous jaw and extremely small forearms

Also available from Borealis:
Triceratops • Parasaurolophus

Helicopters were used to shoot the footage for Soarin' Around the World.

THE NUMBER

1928

IS ON SEVERAL BUILDINGS IN DISNEY'S HOLLYWOOD STUDIOS—THAT'S THE YEAR OF THE FIRST MICKEY MOUSE CARTOON.

A floral sculpture of Mickey Mouse in Dubai Miracle Garden, in the **UNITED ARAB EMIRATES**, is about as tall as a **SIX-STORY BUILDING**.

The **AQUADUCK** on the *Disney Dream* cruise ship was the first water coaster at sea.

Riders tube over the edge of the ship and back, **SWOOSHING** past four decks.

57

A chimpanzee carving on the
Tree of Life
at Disney's Animal Kingdom
is of **David Greybeard,**
the first chimp observed
using a tool
in the wild.

Primatologist **Jane Goodall** named him, and his is the **only carving** on the tree that's modeled after an individual animal.

THE SLINKY DOG DASH COASTER at Disney's Hollywood Studios **stops during the ride** and then sends you over a hill, a design crafted to imitate a **pull-back-and-launch toy.**

The **Dumbo octopus** is named for the large, earlike fins that it uses to move through the water.

FOR THE OPENING SCENE IN THE LAND OF THE DEAD IN *COCO* (2017), ANIMATORS CREATED **8.5 MILLION LIGHTS.**

COREY THE MANTICORE IN *ONWARD* (2020) IS A COMBINATION OF A LION, A SCORPION, A BAT, AND A HUMAN.

To celebrate the release of *Maleficent* (2014), a world-record number of people dressed as princesses gathered outside a theater in England.

Artists carved concrete using crumpled aluminum foil to create the craggy look of the Himalaya mountains at Disney's Animal Kingdom.

In 2018, one woman set a world record by visiting all 12 Disney theme parks, and going on at least one attraction in each, in 75 hours 6 minutes.

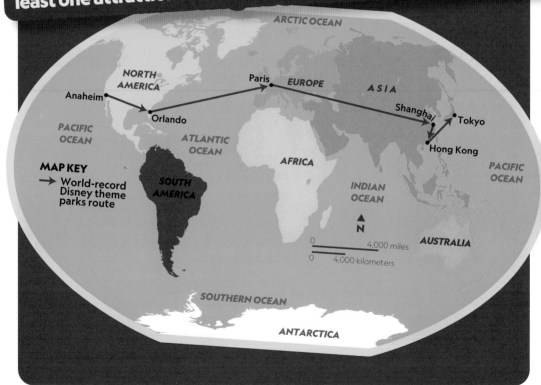

ARCTIC OCEAN

NORTH AMERICA

Anaheim

Orlando

PACIFIC OCEAN

ATLANTIC OCEAN

Paris   EUROPE

ASIA

Shanghai   Tokyo

Hong Kong

AFRICA

PACIFIC OCEAN

MAP KEY

→ World-record Disney theme parks route

SOUTH AMERICA

INDIAN OCEAN

N

AUSTRALIA

0   4,000 miles
0   4,000 kilometers

SOUTHERN OCEAN

ANTARCTICA

To celebrate Disneyland's **50th anniversary** in 2005, vehicles from opening-day attractions were painted **gold.**

BUZZ LIGHTYEAR from *Toy Story* (1995) was named for astronaut BUZZ ALDRIN, who was one of the first two people to walk on the moon.

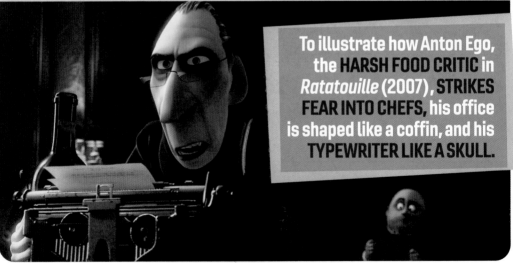

To illustrate how Anton Ego, the HARSH FOOD CRITIC in *Ratatouille* (2007), STRIKES FEAR INTO CHEFS, his office is shaped like a coffin, and his TYPEWRITER LIKE A SKULL.

Bill Clinton was the first U.S. president to provide his voice for his Audio-Animatronics® figure in the Hall of Presidents at the Magic Kingdom.

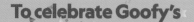

To celebrate Goofy's **90th birthday** in 2022, one woman set a record for collecting the largest number of Goofy memorabilia— **1,825 items.**

Walt Disney's teacher asked his class to draw flowers; Disney's had human faces and arms with hands.

THE **TELEGRAPH CODE** HEARD AT THE DISNEYLAND RAILROAD'S NEW ORLEANS SQUARE STATION **SPELLS OUT** WALT DISNEY'S SPEECH ON THE PARK'S **OPENING DAY,** JULY 17, 1955.

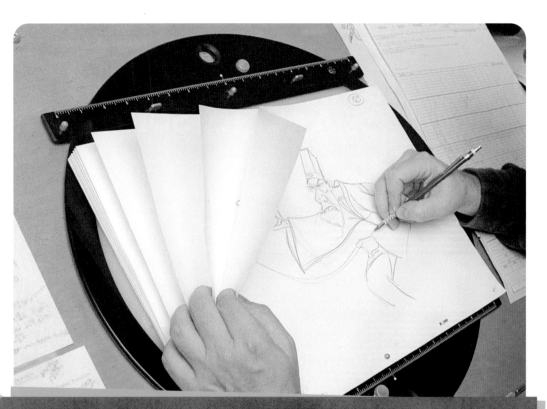

It takes **1,440 separate sketches** to create **one minute** of hand-drawn animation.

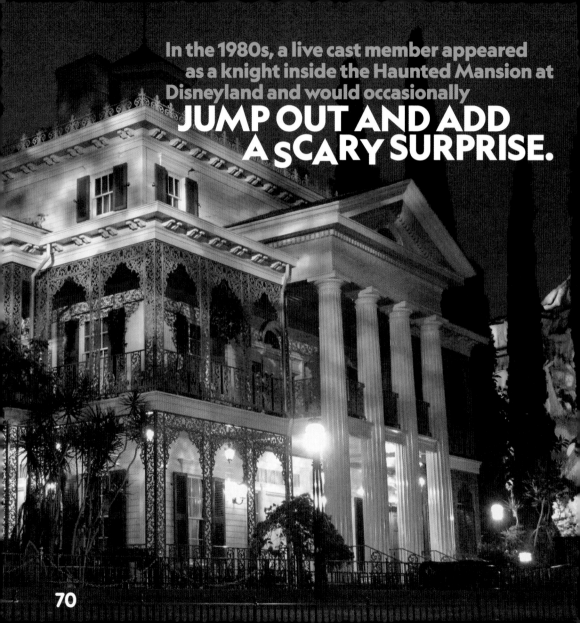

In the 1980s, a live cast member appeared as a knight inside the Haunted Mansion at Disneyland and would occasionally **JUMP OUT AND ADD A SCARY SURPRISE.**

There are

13
candles
on the **birthday cake** in the **ballroom** at the
Haunted Mansion.

Toy Story (1995) animators studied the movements of the Scarecrow in *The Wizard of Oz* (1939) as an example of how a stuffed character, like Woody, could **flop** **and** **bend.**

The **Pumpkin Trees** on each of the **Disney Cruise Line ships,** which only **"blossom"** during the Halloween season, are named **Grim, Mucklebones, Bog, Reap, and Boo.**

THE CHRISTMAS TREE DISPLAYED IN TOWN SQUARE AT THE MAGIC KINGDOM **WEIGHS 16.5 TONS** (15 T) AND IS STRUNG WITH **5,400 LIGHTS.**

THE **OLDEST OBJECT** AT DISNEYLAND IS A **75-MILLION-YEAR-OLD** PETRIFIED TREE.

FOR A **Halloween celebration** AT DISNEYLAND IN 1995, CAST MEMBERS CARVED A PUMPKIN THAT WEIGHED **516 POUNDS** (234 KG)— ABOUT AS MUCH AS A **SIBERIAN TIGER.**

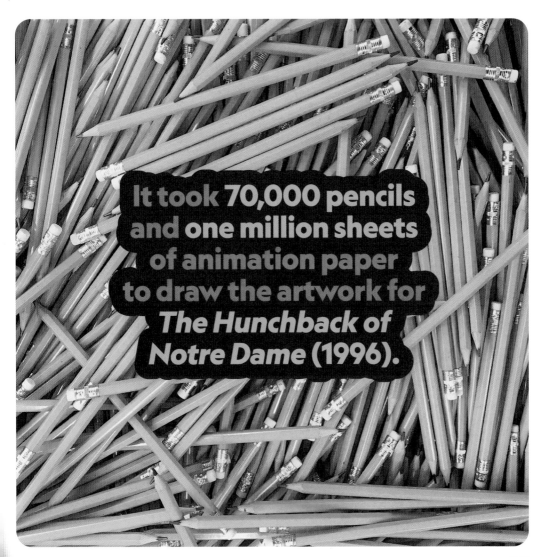

It took **70,000 pencils** and **one million sheets** of animation paper to draw the artwork for *The Hunchback of Notre Dame* (1996).

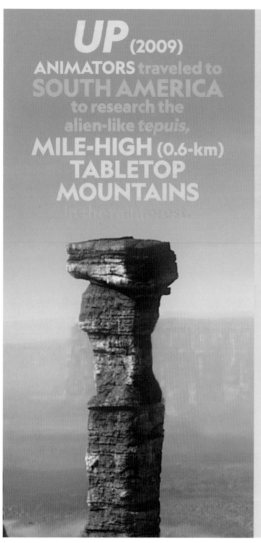

UP (2009)

ANIMATORS traveled to **SOUTH AMERICA** to research the alien-like *tepuis,* **MILE-HIGH** (0.6-km) **TABLETOP MOUNTAINS** in the rainforest.

To understand how the **Green Army Soldiers** would move in the Toy Story movies, animators **stuck shoes on a board** and then walked in them.

Walt Disney would often **stand in line** with his guests at Disneyland while they **waited to board a ride.**

The **LIGHTHOUSE** built for *Pete's Dragon* (1977) was so authentic that the film crew had to get **PERMISSION FROM THE UNITED STATES COAST GUARD** to use it.

Goat horns were the inspiration for Maleficent's headdress in *Sleeping Beauty* (1959).

AFRICA'S AFAR DEPRESSION, WITH ITS SALT FLATS AND STEAM-SPEWING LIMESTONE CHIMNEYS, WAS THE INSPIRATION FOR THE HYENAS' HIDEOUT IN *THE LION KING* (2019).

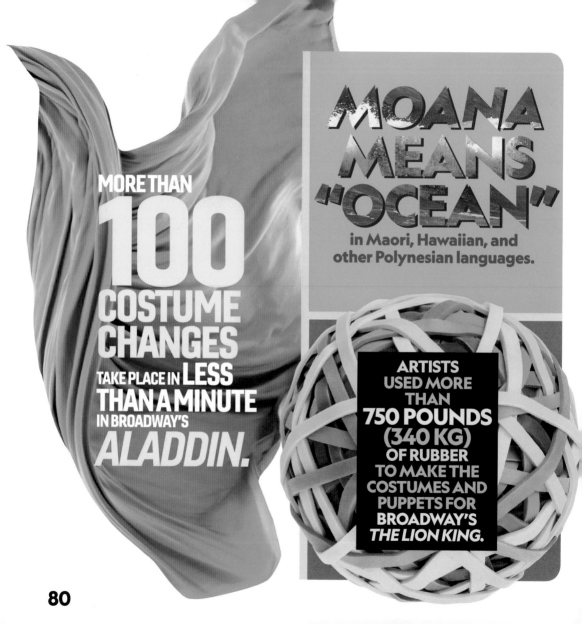

MORE THAN 100 COSTUME CHANGES TAKE PLACE IN **LESS THAN A MINUTE** IN BROADWAY'S *ALADDIN.*

MOANA MEANS "OCEAN" in Maori, Hawaiian, and other Polynesian languages.

ARTISTS USED MORE THAN 750 POUNDS (340 KG) OF RUBBER TO MAKE THE COSTUMES AND PUPPETS FOR BROADWAY'S *THE LION KING.*

Animators for *Bolt* (2008) had a pet hamster named

Doink!

that helped them model the movements for the animated hamster Rhino.

Anika Noni Rose, who voiced

TIANA

in *The Princess and the Frog* (2009), asked that her character be **LEFT-HANDED, JUST LIKE HER.**

FOR *SECRETS OF THE WHALES* (2021), SCIENTISTS COLLECTED MORE DATA ON THESE SEA MAMMALS THAN THE HUBBLE TELESCOPE GATHERS ABOUT SPACE IN A YEAR.

There are more than **10,000 items** in the antiques mall that Woody wanders in *Toy Story 4* (2019).

EACH OF THE MORE THAN **270 FOOD ITEMS** THAT APPEAR IN *RATATOUILLE* (2007) WAS PREPARED IN A REAL KITCHEN AND EATEN.

Rafiki— the name of the mandrill in *The Lion King* (1994)—means "friend" in Swahili.

An actor **growled** into a trash can to **create** the lion roars for the film.

85

THE **PUMBAA COSTUME** IN BROADWAY'S *THE LION KING* WEIGHS **45 POUNDS (20 KG)** AND IS WORN LIKE A **BACKPACK.**

Only materials that would have been available on **Pacific islands** were used to design the characters' clothes in *Moana* (2016).

IN 1933, MICKEY MOUSE REPORTEDLY RECEIVED **800,000 FAN LETTERS,** THE MOST OF ANY HOLLYWOOD STAR AT THE TIME.

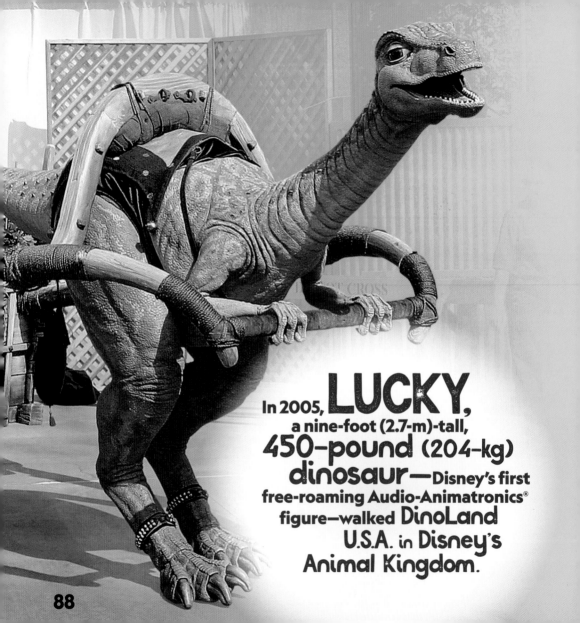

In 2005, **LUCKY,** a nine-foot (2.7-m)-tall, **450-pound (204-kg) dinosaur—Disney's first free-roaming Audio-Animatronics® figure—walked DinoLand U.S.A. in Disney's Animal Kingdom.**

The 82-foot (25-m)-tall fireplace in **DISNEY'S WILDERNESS LODGE**

mimics the layers of the Grand Canyon, which represent **1.6 BILLION YEARS OF GEOLOGIC HISTORY.**

MAYOR LIONHEART FROM *ZOOTOPIA* (2016) WAS PARTLY INSPIRED BY *THE LION KING'S* **MUFASA.**

AROUND HALLOWEEN, MORE THAN
300 SCULPTED PUMPKINS
LINE MAIN STREET, U.S.A. AT DISNEYLAND—AND NO TWO ARE ALIKE.

Walt Disney decided to make a **Winnie the Pooh film** after hearing his children **giggle** while listening to A. A. Milne's Winnie-the-Pooh stories.

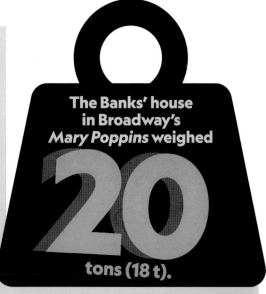

The Banks' house in Broadway's *Mary Poppins* weighed **20** tons (18 t).

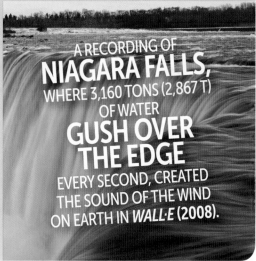

A RECORDING OF **NIAGARA FALLS,** WHERE 3,160 TONS (2,867 T) OF WATER **GUSH OVER THE EDGE** EVERY SECOND, CREATED THE SOUND OF THE WIND ON EARTH IN *WALL·E* (2008).

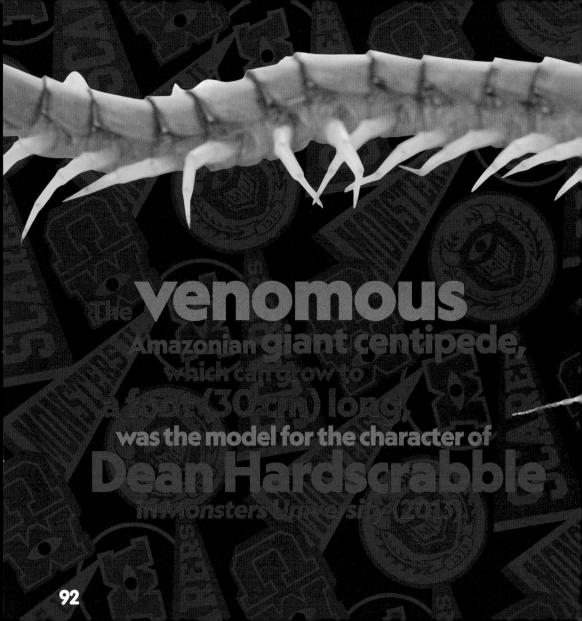

The **venomous** Amazonian **giant centipede,** which can grow to a foot (30 cm) long, was the model for the character of **Dean Hardscrabble** in *Monsters University* (2013).

The gargoyles of Notre Dame Cathedral partly inspired the Beast's castle in *Beauty and the Beast* (1991).

In the film, Belle is the only character in her village who wears the color blue.

Finnick's name in *Zootopia* (2016) is a play on his species, the fennec fox.

THE **MAKEUP** FOR EACH OF **BLACKBEARD'S ZOMBIE CREW** IN *PIRATES OF THE CARIBBEAN: ON STRANGER TIDES* (2011) TOOK AN AVERAGE OF **THREE AND A HALF HOURS** TO COMPLETE.

THE LARGE **MR. POTATO HEAD** outside Toy Story Midway Mania! at Disney California Adventure can say more lines than any other Disney-created **AUDIO-ANIMATRONICS® FIGURE.**

In one year, each **Radiator Springs Racers ride vehicle travels about 36,000 miles** (57,936 km)—that's equal to almost one and a half trips around the Equator.

The **23** on the 623 trolley at Disney California Adventure refers to **1923**, the year Walt Disney **arrived** in Los Angeles.

The carvings above The Little Mermaid ~ Ariel's Undersea Adventure at Disney California Adventure depict Ariel's six older sisters: **Aquata, Andrina, Arista, Attina, Adella,** and **Alana.**

You can buy a soap pump that dispenses soap in the shape of Mickey Mouse's head.

The Anaheim Fire Department thought the burning city scene in Pirates of the Caribbean looked so real that they were reluctant to approve the ride.

ONE WOMAN OWNS MORE THAN **10,000 ITEMS OF MICKEY MOUSE MEMORABILIA—** THE WORLD'S LARGEST COLLECTION.

The attraction "it's a small world" is found at Disney parks on three continents—North America, Europe, and Asia—so its theme song is always playing somewhere on Earth.

More than **3,600 colorful plants** create Mickey Mouse's floral face at the entrance to Disneyland.

AT CLUB COOL

IN **WORLD CELEBRATION** AT EPCOT, YOU CAN TASTE-TEST SODAS FROM AROUND THE WORLD.

CAPUCHIN MONKEYS

AT THE LOS ANGELES ZOO WERE PART OF THE INSPIRATION FOR **ABU** IN *ALADDIN (1992)*.

100

One person's sole job at Disneyland is to take care of **King Arthur Carrousel's 68 horses,** many of which are more than **100 years old.**

The **windows and interior handles** of the monorail cars at Tokyo Disney Resort are shaped like **Mickey Mouse's head.**

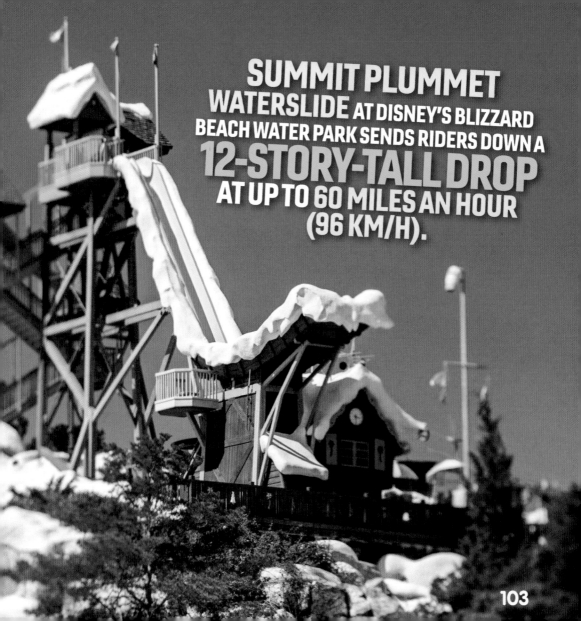

SUMMIT PLUMMET WATERSLIDE AT DISNEY'S BLIZZARD BEACH WATER PARK SENDS RIDERS DOWN A **12-STORY-TALL DROP** AT UP TO 60 MILES AN HOUR (96 KM/H).

THE TREASURE SCENE IN DISNEYLAND'S PIRATES OF THE CARIBBEAN ATTRACTION CONTAINS ABOUT **400,000 COINS.**

A113

In almost every **Pixar film,** viewers can spot "A113," which is the **number of a classroom** at California Institute of the Arts (CalArts) where some **Pixar animators studied.**

In the **Toy Story Midway Mania!** attraction, **virtual balloons "pop"** with real blasts of air.

TO HELP ANIMATORS STAGE THE ACTION FOR *SNOW WHITE AND THE SEVEN DWARFS* (1937), A DISNEY ARTIST CREATED A FULL-SCALE MODEL OF THE **DWARFS' COTTAGE.**

MICKEY MOUSE'S BIRTHDAY IS NOVEMBER 18, THE DAY THAT "STEAMBOAT WILLIE" (1928), HIS AND MINNIE'S FIRST CARTOON, PREMIERED.

THE MOTION OF A RATTLESNAKE STRIKING WAS THE INSPIRATION FOR THE **DRAGON** MOVING TO ATTACK PRINCE PHILLIP IN *SLEEPING BEAUTY* (1959).

NATIONAL DONALD DUCK DAY IS JUNE 9, THE DAY HIS FIRST CARTOON, "THE WISE LITTLE HEN" (1934), PREMIERED.

Much of "it's a small world" was designed to look like a child's papier-mâché art project.

THE FIRST ANIMAL BORN AT DISNEY'S ANIMAL KINGDOM WAS A **KUDU,** A LARGE AFRICAN ANTELOPE.

Some popcorn carts at Disneyland feature "Roastie-Toasties"— dolls that rotate the popcorn drums.

In the "It's Tough to be a Bug!" 3D film at Disney's Animal Kingdom, **visitors smell the stench of a stink bug.**

It takes 70,000 "perfume" pellets to create the smell.

THE DESIGN OF THE LIFEBOATS ON DISNEY CRUISE LINE SHIPS IS INSPIRED BY THE **COLOR OF MICKEY MOUSE'S SHOES.**

❤ 1M

ONE MILLION PEOPLE
VISITED DISNEYLAND IN THE FIRST SEVEN WEEKS IT WAS OPEN.

OUT

The Guardians of the Galaxy: Cosmic Rewind coaster at EPCOT includes a backward launch, and the ride vehicles turn 360 degrees.

As a boy, Walt Disney drew on anything he could find—even toilet paper.

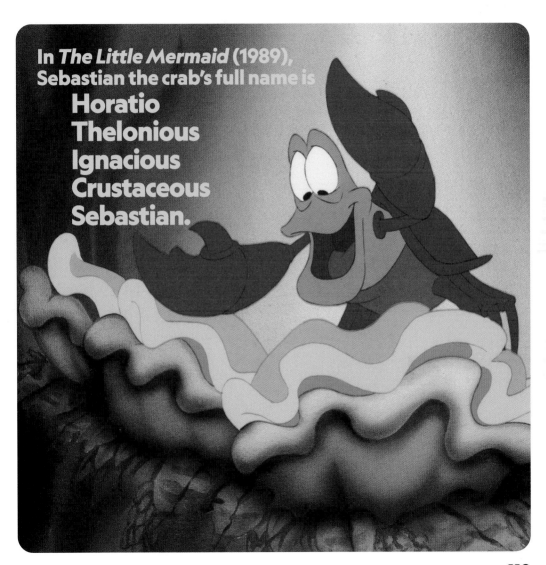

In *The Little Mermaid* (1989), Sebastian the crab's full name is **Horatio Thelonious Ignacious Crustaceous Sebastian.**

THE singing busts IN THE HAUNTED MANSION ARE NAMED ...

ROLO RUMKIN

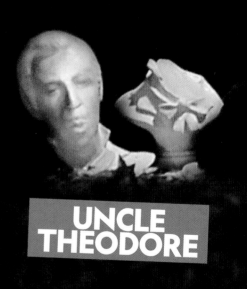

UNCLE THEODORE

COUSIN
ALGERNON

NED
NUB

PHINEAS
P. POCK

Cinderella's dress **transforming into a ball gown** was said to be Walt Disney's favorite piece of animation.

Walt Disney's pocket on the "Storytellers" statue in Disney California Adventure

holds the *Kansas City Star* newspaper— a nod to the city where

Walt opened his first animation studio.

At the France pavilion in EPCOT, some of the manhole covers feature Remy from *Ratatouille* (2007), a reference to the rat's arrival in Paris via the sewers.

The Forbidden Mountain at Disney's Animal Kingdom is the tallest "mountain" in Florida, at almost 200 feet (61 m).

WHEN THE **JUNGLE CRUISE** WAS BUILT AT DISNEYLAND, ORANGE TREES WERE PLANTED UPSIDE DOWN BECAUSE THEIR **ROOTS LOOKED LIKE A TYPE OF TREE FROM AFRICA.**

More than half the U.S. population watched the television broadcast of Disneyland's opening day on July 17, 1955.

Donald Duck has an asteroid named after him.

The movements of **Baymax,** the inflatable robot in *Big Hero 6* (2014), were based on those of **baby penguins.**

Mirabel from *Encanto* (2021) is the first Disney female lead character to **wear glasses.**

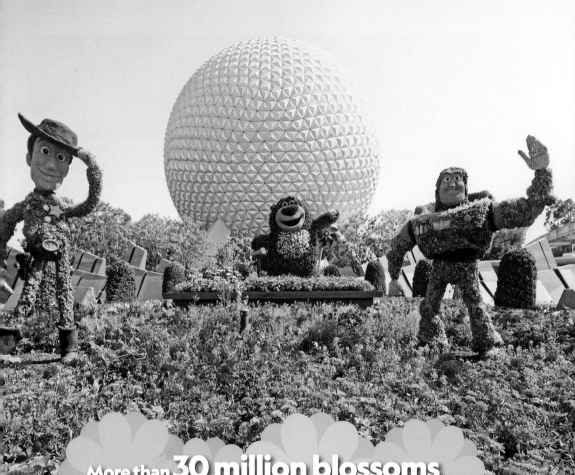

More than **30 million blossoms** bloom at the EPCOT International Flower & Garden Festival.

Main Street, U.S.A. is partly based on **1910** America and Tomorrowland on **1986**, the only two years in the 20th century that **Halley's comet** streaked across the skies.

EACH RIDE SYSTEM ON **MISSION: SPACE** HAS MORE COMPUTING POWER THAN A **SPACE SHUTTLE.**

WALT DISNEY LOVED TRAINS SO MUCH THAT HE HAD ONE IN HIS BACKYARD BIG ENOUGH FOR HIM TO RIDE.

Sleeping Beauty Castle opened in 1955, more than three years before the release of *Sleeping Beauty* (1959).

Gustave Eiffel's blueprints were used to create the Eiffel Tower in the France pavilion at **EPCOT.**

BRUCE, THE GREAT WHITE SHARK IN *FINDING NEMO* (2003), HAS **202 TEETH** THAT ARE EACH ANIMATABLE.

MICKEY MOUSE
is called
Topolino
in Italy and
Musse Pigg
in Sweden.

SANTA SHARES 300 POUNDS (136 KG)

OF GINGERBREAD COOKIES ON EACH

DISNEY CRUISE LINE SHIP DURING THE HOLIDAYS.

KEVIN in *Up* (2009) is a combination of many birds, including a

cassowary,

an ostrich,

and a monal pheasant.

GOLDEN MONKEYS,

ASIAN LANGURS, AND PREHISTORIC *GIGANTOPITHECUS*—THE BIGGEST PRIMATE THAT EVER LIVED—WERE AMONG THE INSPIRATIONS FOR THE **Yeti in Expedition Everest** — LEGEND OF THE FORBIDDEN MOUNTAIN.

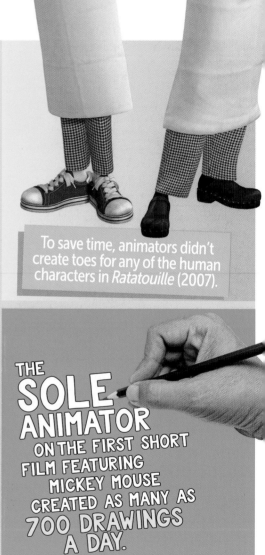

To save time, animators didn't create toes for any of the human characters in *Ratatouille* (2007).

THE SOLE ANIMATOR
ON THE FIRST SHORT FILM FEATURING MICKEY MOUSE CREATED AS MANY AS **700 DRAWINGS A DAY.**

ANIMATORS CREATED ALMOST 13,000 INDIVIDUAL CORALS FOR NEMO AND HIS FRIENDS TO SWIM THROUGH IN *FINDING NEMO* (2003).

To make Miguel's homemade guitar more realistically childlike, the director of *Coco* (2017) asked his son to design it.

Some of the cobblestones in the streets of *Coco's* (2017) Land of the Dead are bone-shaped.

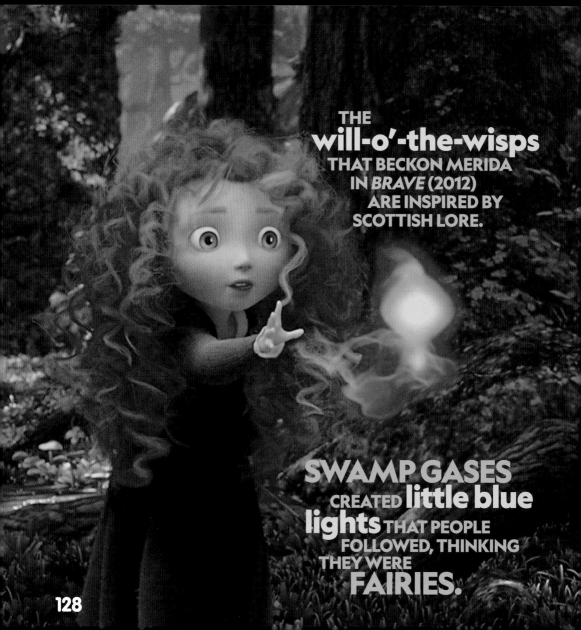

THE **will-o'-the-wisps** THAT BECKON MERIDA IN *BRAVE* (2012) ARE INSPIRED BY SCOTTISH LORE.

SWAMP GASES CREATED **little blue lights** THAT PEOPLE FOLLOWED, THINKING THEY WERE **FAIRIES.**

The **Pizza Planet truck,** which first appeared in *Toy Story* (1995), appears in almost every **Pixar movie.**

The Fantasmic! show features scenes from Disney movies projected onto screens of water.

There is a restaurant inside the **Pirates of the Caribbean** attraction at Disneyland.

IN *SOUL* (2020), THE NUMBER OF SOULS WHO LEAVE THE GREAT BEFORE FOR EARTH IS BASED ON REAL STATISTICS:

About **four people** are born each second around the world.

Guests of Disneyland Resort Hotels can sign up for an EARLY MORNING POWER WALK through Disney California Adventure before the park opens.

Mickey Mouse wears more than 200 outfits at Disneyland Paris.

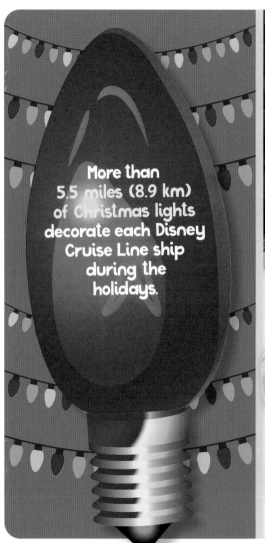

More than 5.5 miles (8.9 km) of Christmas lights decorate each Disney Cruise Line ship during the holidays.

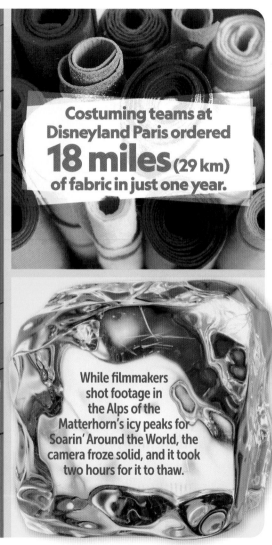

Costuming teams at Disneyland Paris ordered **18 miles** (29 km) of fabric in just one year.

While filmmakers shot footage in the Alps of the Matterhorn's icy peaks for Soarin' Around the World, the camera froze solid, and it took two hours for it to thaw.

WHEN CREATING THE CHARACTER OF **ARLO**

FOR *THE GOOD DINOSAUR* (2015), ANIMATORS VISITED A ZOO TO WATCH HOW ELEPHANTS—ANOTHER HEAVY, FOUR-FOOTED ANIMAL—MOVED.

135

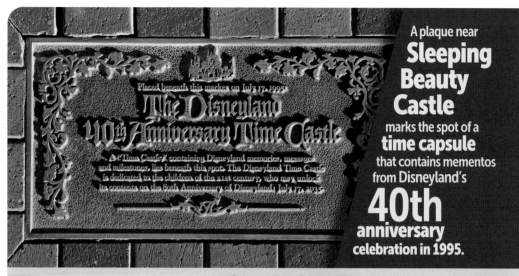

Placed beneath this marker on July 17, 1995.

The Disneyland 40th Anniversary Time Castle

A "Time Castle," containing Disneyland memories, messages and milestones, lies beneath this spot. The Disneyland Time Castle is dedicated to the children of the 21st century, who may unlock its contents on the 80th Anniversary of Disneyland, July 17, 2035.

A plaque near **Sleeping Beauty Castle** marks the spot of a **time capsule** that contains mementos from Disneyland's **40th** anniversary celebration in 1995.

At the opening of **"it's a small world"** at Disneyland in 1966, **Walt Disney** and a group of children poured water collected from **Earth's rivers and oceans** into the ride's canal.

Grizzly Peak at Disney California Adventure is in the form of a California grizzly bear— the state animal.

The main courtyard of Disney's **Hollywood Studios** forms a **big Hidden Mickey** that can only be seen from above.

137

The actor who played the **Beast in Beauty and the Beast** (2017) walked on stilts and wore a **40-POUND** (18-KG) **SUIT** with movement sensors to create the computer-generated character.

Walt Disney originally wanted **real animals** to entertain guests on the **Jungle Cruise.**

Monsters, Inc. Mike & Sulley to the Rescue! at Disney California Adventure takes guests through the middle of a bathroom.

At the Disneyland Resort, used **cooking oil is converted into biodiesel** to fuel the steam trains and the Mark Twain Riverboat.

Pixar Pal-A-Round at Disney California Adventure is a full-size reproduction of a Ferris wheel that was built in 1920 and still operates in Coney Island, New York, U.S.A.

The **T. rex family** in *The Good Dinosaur* (2015) **are ranchers,** so animators gave them lower bodies that move like **galloping horses** and upper bodies of **riding cowboys.**

To make the New York City scenes realistic, *Soul* (2020) animators included black spots on the sidewalks to look like wads of walked-over chewing gum.

NORTH AMERICA

ASIA

EUROPE

EUROPE
Italy

AFRICA

EUROPE

Maranello

ITALY

Adriatic Sea

Tyrrhenian Sea

Mediterranean Sea

AFRICA

Sulley

in *Monsters, Inc.* (2001) has more than five million individual hairs on his body.

IN *CARS* (2006), LUIGI'S LICENSE PLATE NUMBER,

·44.5-10.8,

REPRESENTS THE LATITUDE AND LONGITUDE OF **FERRARI HEADQUARTERS** IN MARANELLO, ITALY.

Lilo & Stitch (2002) animators consulted Hawaiian hula

dancers to make sure that Lilo's hula steps were accurate.

For *Onward* (2020), animators danced with their arms tied behind their backs to create footage for **the moving pair of pants.**

The PINOCCHIO LIZARD, which has a long nose, is named after the puppet whose nose grows when he lies.

Paradise Falls in *Up* (2009) is based on **Venezuela's** **Angel Falls,** the world's tallest waterfall.

147

The manatees at The Seas with Nemo & Friends at EPCOT eat more than 100 heads of lettuce a day.

Gino, a silverback gorilla at Disney's Animal Kingdom, celebrated his 41st birthday with a cake made of alfalfa, banana leaves, and sweet potato frosting.

Two actors who voiced Mickey Mouse and Minnie Mouse were married to each other in real life.

WHEN WALT DISNEY WAS THINKING ABOUT A NAME FOR WHAT WOULD BECOME DISNEYLAND, HE CONSIDERED CALLING IT "MICKEY MOUSE PARK."

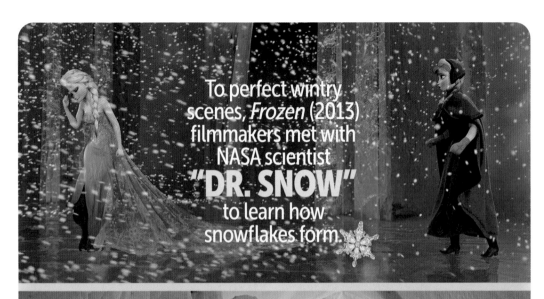

To perfect wintry scenes, *Frozen* (2013) filmmakers met with NASA scientist **"DR. SNOW"** to learn how snowflakes form.

Québec City's **HÔTEL DE GLACE,** where you can **sleep in a room made of snow and ice,** was an inspiration for Elsa's ice palace in *Frozen* (2013).

REINDEER use their hind legs to scratch their ears—a trait that *Frozen* (2013) animators used for the character of **SVEN.**

Disneynature filmmakers **TRAVELED ACROSS A GLACIER FOR 10 DAYS** to transport the sled-mounted mobile camp they lived in while filming the documentary *POLAR BEAR* (2022).

HIPPOS at Disney's Animal Kingdom sometimes get WHOLE WATERMELONS as treats when learning how to open their mouths for dental checkups.

MEERKATS have such a tight-knit social structure that when one needs a checkup at Disney's Animal Kingdom, the WHOLE FAMILY typically goes to the vet.

Mirrors are sometimes used in the **LESSER FLAMINGO** exhibits at Disney's Animal Kingdom to create the illusion of the larger flocks that these birds would be part of during breeding season in the wild.

ROCK 'N' ROLLER COASTER STARRING **AEROSMITH** WAS THE FIRST COASTER AT WALT DISNEY WORLD TO TAKE GUESTS UPSIDE DOWN.

PHINEAS, EZRA, AND GUS are the names of the HITCHHIKING GHOSTS who try to catch a ride out of the Haunted Mansion.

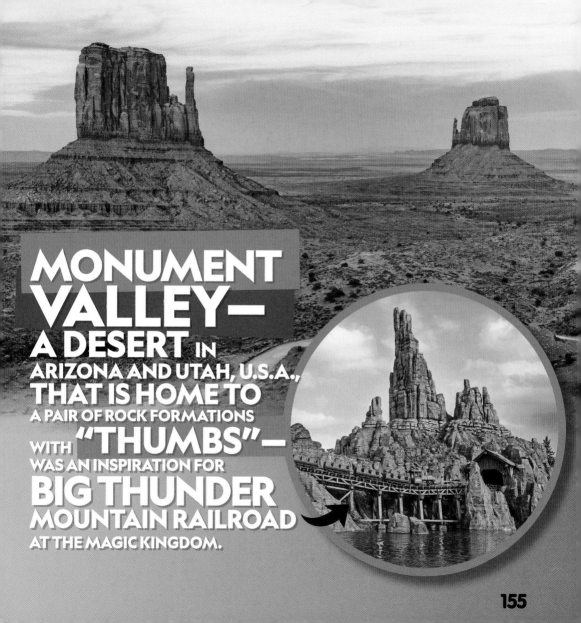

MONUMENT VALLEY— A DESERT IN ARIZONA AND UTAH, U.S.A., THAT IS HOME TO A PAIR OF ROCK FORMATIONS WITH **"THUMBS"—** WAS AN INSPIRATION FOR **BIG THUNDER MOUNTAIN RAILROAD** AT THE MAGIC KINGDOM.

Disneynature filmmakers **wore penguin masks** to blend in with **Earth's largest Adélie colony**—more than **one million birds in Antarctica**—while shooting the documentary *Penguins* (2019).

The ball gown for *Cinderella* (2015) was made with about three miles (4.8 km) of thread in the hem alone, eight silk skirts, and more than 11,000 crystals.

THE ACTRESS WHO PLAYED CINDERELLA DID NOT WALK IN THE **CRYSTAL HEELS** CREATED FOR THE FILM—

SHE WORE LEATHER SHOES AND A COMPUTER MADE THEM APPEAR AS THE **GLASS SLIPPERS.**

The **murals in Cinderella Castle** at the Magic Kingdom are made with hundreds of thousands of glass tiles in **500 colors,** including a **red shade** made just for Cinderella's **jealous stepsister.**

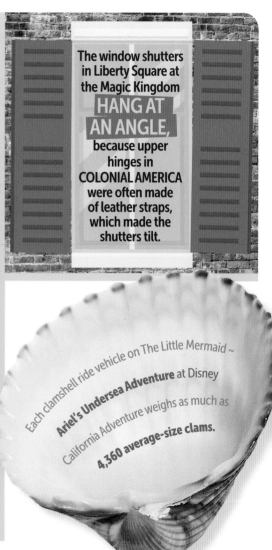

The window shutters in Liberty Square at the Magic Kingdom **HANG AT AN ANGLE,** because upper hinges in **COLONIAL AMERICA** were often made of leather straps, which made the shutters tilt.

Each clamshell ride vehicle on The Little Mermaid ~ **Ariel's Undersea Adventure** at Disney California Adventure weighs as much as **4,360 average-size clams.**

A police escort helps transport about 100 tons (91 t) of holiday decorations to Main Street, U.S.A. at the Magic Kingdom each year.

During the **holidays,** each of the more than **300 dolls** in "it's a small world" at Disneyland is dressed in a **special costume or accessory.**

FILMMAKERS **STUDIED** THE **LIONS** AT **DISNEY'S ANIMAL KINGDOM** TO CREATE *THE LION KING'S* **COMPUTER-GENERATED ONES.**

SPECIAL **"GROOM" ARTISTS** CREATED THE REALISTIC LOOK OF THE ANIMALS' **FUR** IN *THE LION KING* (2019).

Walt Disney himself suggested that the "Jolly Holiday" waiters in *Mary Poppins* (1964) should be animated penguins.

SOME OF THE **COSTUMES FOR *MULAN*** (1998) WERE INSPIRED BY THE **8,000** LIFE-SIZE TERRA-COTTA WARRIORS FOUND IN THE MAUSOLEUM OF A CHINESE EMPEROR.

To make the posters that hang in the middle school in **Turning Red (2022)** look as if they were

drawn by middle schoolers,

some artists changed their **grip on their pen.**

IMAGINEERS MIXED CONCRETE WITH STONES, DIRT, AND TWIGS TO CREATE THE **BUMPY ROAD** FOR THE KILIMANJARO SAFARIS IN DISNEY'S ANIMAL KINGDOM.

An artist who helped **restore the stained-glass windows for Notre Dame Cathedral** also designed the windows for Sleeping Beauty Castle at Disneyland Paris.

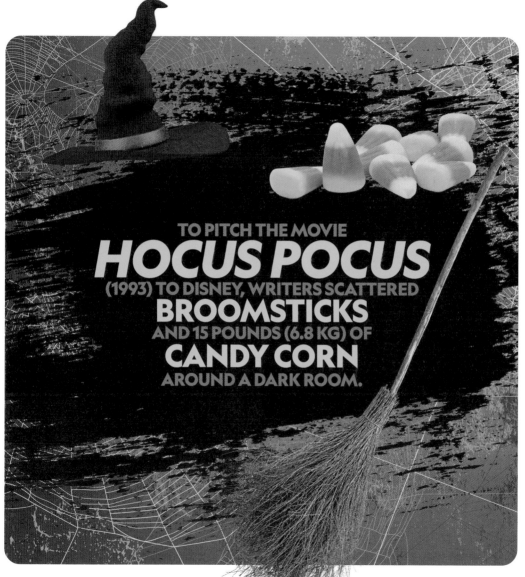

TO PITCH THE MOVIE
HOCUS POCUS
(1993) TO DISNEY, WRITERS SCATTERED
BROOMSTICKS
AND 15 POUNDS (6.8 KG) OF
CANDY CORN
AROUND A DARK ROOM.

In *Wreck-It Ralph* (2012), the high score of the Fix-It Felix Jr. video game, 120501, refers to Walt Disney's birthday: December 5, 1901.

SCIENTISTS SUGGESTED **ASTROTURF** FOR THE HABITAT OF HANK, THE OCTOPUS IN *FINDING DORY* (2016)—IT WOULD PREVENT HIS ESCAPE BECAUSE HIS SUCKERS COULDN'T STICK TO IT.

The tree house in **Swiss Family Robinson** (1960) was built in a **200-foot** (61-m)-tall **saman tree** in Tobago.

THE NAUTILUS, CAPTAIN NEMO'S SHIP IN *20,000 LEAGUES UNDER THE SEA* (1954), WAS DESIGNED TO RESEMBLE A CROSS BETWEEN ...

AN ALLIGATOR

AND A SHARK.

The clicking steps of the pet Cockroach in *WALL·E* (2008) are a recording of handcuffs jingling.

1,428

Swarovski diamonds
were sewn into just
**ONE PAIR OF
COSTUME PANTS**
worn in Broadway's *Aladdin.*

Prince Charming does not have a given name in _Cinderella_ (1950).

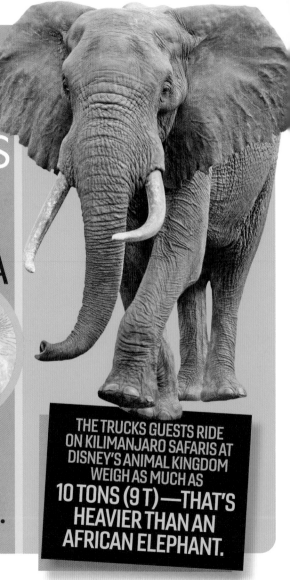

SCIENTISTS NAMED ONE SPECIES OF A TINY FAIRY FLY *TINKERBELLA NANA,* AFTER TWO CHARACTERS IN *PETER PAN* (1953).

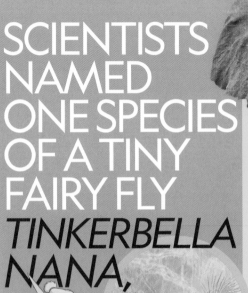

THE TRUCKS GUESTS RIDE ON KILIMANJARO SAFARIS AT DISNEY'S ANIMAL KINGDOM WEIGH AS MUCH AS 10 TONS (9 T)—THAT'S HEAVIER THAN AN AFRICAN ELEPHANT.

The **gibbons** at **Disney's Animal Kingdom** sometimes play **matching games** on computer tablets as a form of **mental exercise.**

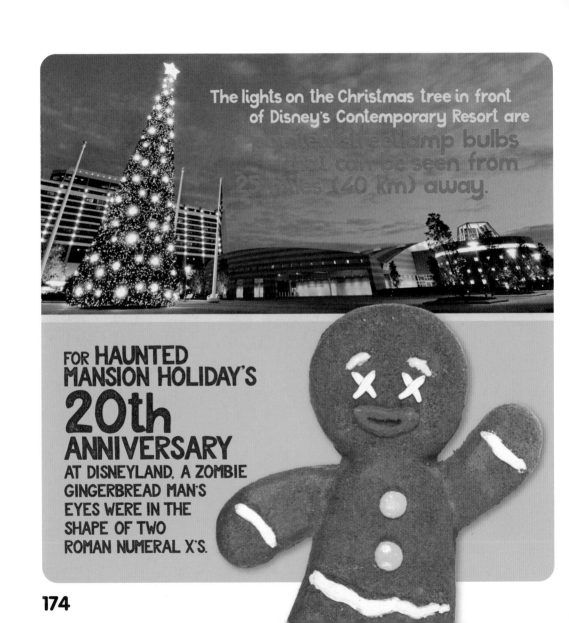

The lights on the Christmas tree in front of Disney's Contemporary Resort are painted streetlamp bulbs that can be seen from 25 miles (40 km) away.

FOR **HAUNTED MANSION HOLIDAY'S**

20th

ANNIVERSARY

AT DISNEYLAND, A ZOMBIE GINGERBREAD MAN'S EYES WERE IN THE SHAPE OF TWO ROMAN NUMERAL X'S.

THE LITTLE MERMAID (1989)
ANIMATORS STUDIED FOOTAGE
OF ASTRONAUT SALLY RIDE
FLOATING IN A SPACE
SHUTTLE TO CREATE
THE MOVEMENT OF
ARIEL'S HAIR UNDERWATER.

175

Lin-Manuel Miranda wrote *Encanto*'s (2021) "Waiting on a Miracle" in a

DIFFERENT
BEAT

from the other songs in the movie to symbolize that Mirabel is an

outsider
in her
family

To research the **dancing animal** scenes in *Fantasia* **(1940),** one animator sat backstage at a ballet production for more than a week and drew **hundreds of sketches.**

SOME AUDIENCES SAW DIFFERENT VERSIONS OF THE ZNN NEWS ANCHOR IN **ZOOTOPIA** (2016): FANS IN CHINA WERE GREETED WITH A PANDA, AND THOSE IN AUSTRALIA, A KOALA.

Main Street Cinema in Disneyland once featured a costumed phantom that would frighten guests.

A snow-simulation model used in the making of *Frozen* (2013) is helping scientists better understand avalanches.

IN MONSTERS, INC. MIKE & SULLEY TO THE RESCUE! THERE ARE 236 DOORS IN THE DOOR VAULT SCENE.

179

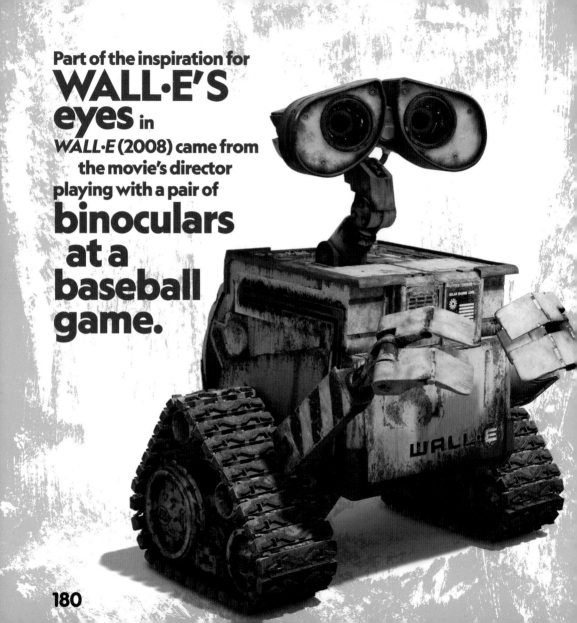

Part of the inspiration for **WALL·E'S eyes** in *WALL·E* (2008) came from the movie's director playing with a pair of **binoculars at a baseball game.**

For a 2004 relay event honoring **Olympic swimmers,** Disneyland cast members **constructed a pool on Main Street, U.S.A.** in less than 30 hours.

TO ENSURE THAT A **RIDE ON SPACE MOUNTAIN** MIMICKED THE FEELING OF BEING IN SPACE, **NASA** ASTRONAUT GORDON COOPER HELPED IMAGINEERS DEVELOP THE COASTER'S CONCEPT.

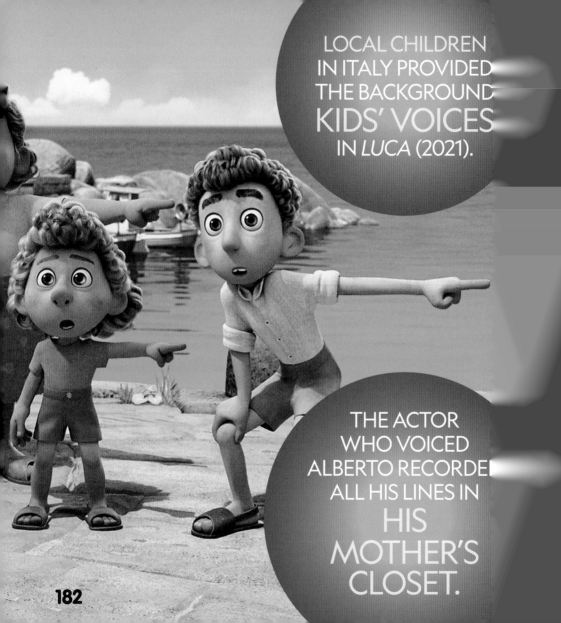

LOCAL CHILDREN IN ITALY PROVIDED THE BACKGROUND KIDS' VOICES IN *LUCA* (2021).

THE ACTOR WHO VOICED ALBERTO RECORDED ALL HIS LINES IN HIS MOTHER'S CLOSET.

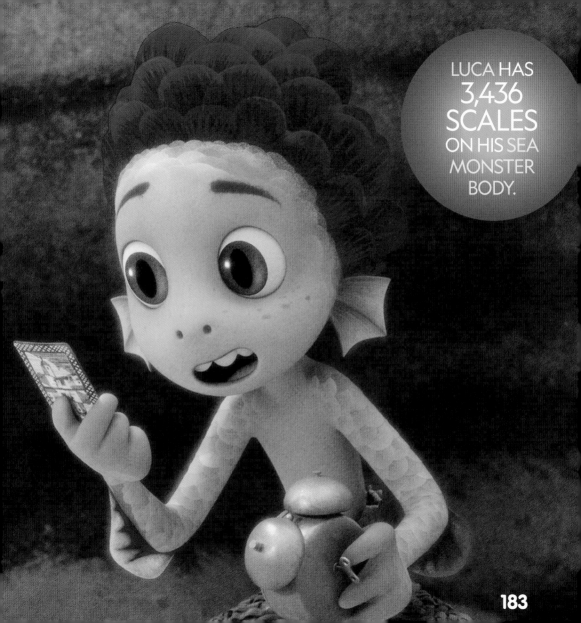

LUCA HAS
3,436
SCALES
ON HIS SEA
MONSTER
BODY.

ON A **SEVEN-NIGHT SAIL** ABOARD THE *DISNEY MAGIC,* **7.5 TONS (6.8 T) OF CHICKEN,** **7.5 TONS (6.8 T) OF MELON,** AND **71,500 EGGS** ARE **EATEN, ON AVERAGE.**

Pixar created a "bug cam" to help animators see the world from a bug's-eye view for *A Bug's Life* (1998).

Guests eat an estimated **1.6 million corn dogs** at Disneyland Resort each year.

Tivoli Gardens in Copenhagen, Denmark, one of the world's oldest amusement parks, was part of **Walt Disney's inspiration for Disneyland.**

PINOCCHIO (1940)
ANIMATORS BUILT REAL MODELS OF SOME OF THE CLOCKS IN GEPPETTO'S WORKSHOP TO SHOW WALT DISNEY THAT THEY COULD ACTUALLY WORK.

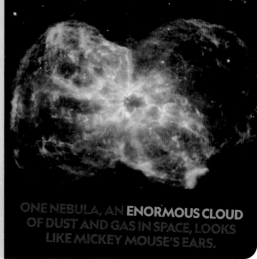

Thousands of bees feast on Walt Disney World Resort's life-size gingerbread houses after the holidays—the sugar keeps them well fed when food is harder to find in the winter.

ONE NEBULA, AN **ENORMOUS CLOUD** OF DUST AND GAS IN SPACE, LOOKS LIKE MICKEY MOUSE'S EARS.

On the set of
Lady and the Tramp
(2019), the dog "stars" had their own trailer for hair and makeup, which included
fake dirt.

187

IT TOOK MORE THAN **500,000 DRAWINGS** **TO ANIMATE ALICE IN WONDERLAND (1951).**

IN THE QUEUE FOR PETER PAN'S FLIGHT IN THE MAGIC KINGDOM, DECEMBER 27 IS CIRCLED ON THE CALENDAR IN THE NURSERY—THAT'S THE DATE J. M. BARRIE'S PLAY *PETER PAN* OPENED IN LONDON.

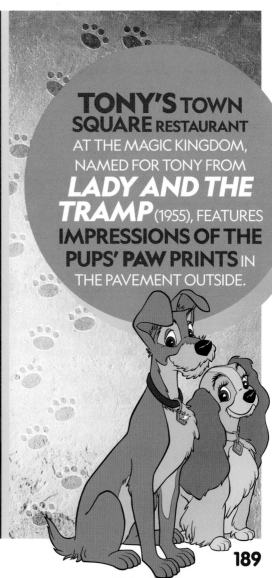

TONY'S TOWN SQUARE RESTAURANT AT THE MAGIC KINGDOM, NAMED FOR TONY FROM *LADY AND THE TRAMP* (1955), FEATURES IMPRESSIONS OF THE PUPS' PAW PRINTS IN THE PAVEMENT OUTSIDE.

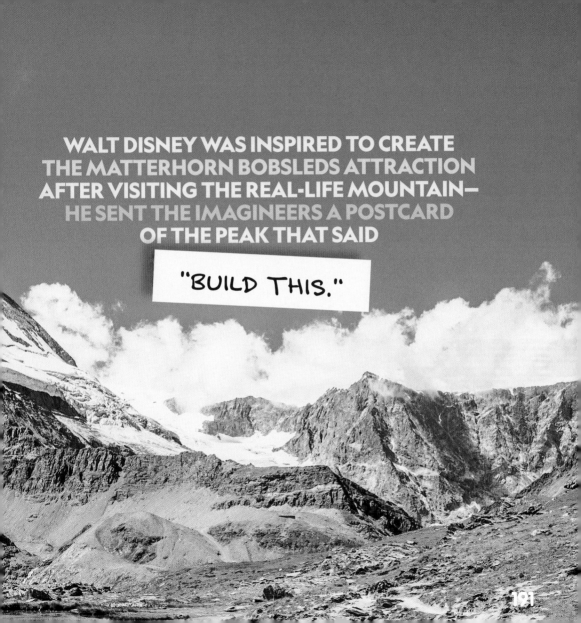

WALT DISNEY WAS INSPIRED TO CREATE
THE MATTERHORN BOBSLEDS ATTRACTION
AFTER VISITING THE REAL-LIFE MOUNTAIN—
HE SENT THE IMAGINEERS A POSTCARD
OF THE PEAK THAT SAID

"BUILD THIS."

The horn signals for Disney Cruise Line ships play the first seven notes of **"When You Wish Upon a Star."**

RAPUNZEL AND FLYNN RIDER FROM *TANGLED* (2010) ATTEND ELSA'S CORONATION IN *FROZEN* (2013).

It took a year to make the 2.5-TON (2.3-T) STAINLESS STEEL PALM TREE that lights the elephant exhibit for the sunset safari at Disney's Animal Kingdom.

YOU CAN FLOAT **400 FEET (122 M) HIGH** IN THE **WORLD'S LARGEST HAND-PAINTED** HELIUM BALLOON AT DISNEY SPRINGS.

Flamethrowers were used to create the **sound of the dragon's fiery breath** in *Sleeping Beauty* (1959).

Visitors to **TIFFINS RESTAURANT** in Disney's Animal Kingdom can see sketches that Imagineers made during their **around-the-world research trips** when planning the park.

THE CAMEL OUTSIDE THE MAGIC CARPETS OF ALADDIN AT THE MAGIC KINGDOM **SPITS,** JUST AS REAL CAMELS DO.

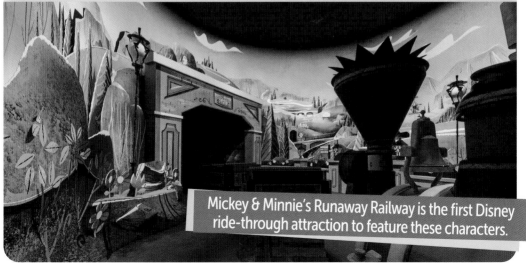

Mickey & Minnie's Runaway Railway is the first Disney ride-through attraction to feature these characters.

The **unique orientation** of the desks in **Mei's classroom** in *Turning Red* (2022) is based on the director's **middle school experience.**

One HIDDEN MICKEY appears only at noon on **NOVEMBER 18, MICKEY'S BIRTHDAY,** when the sun shines through a hole in the QUEUE ROCKWORK at Under the Sea ~ Journey of The Little Mermaid in the MAGIC KINGDOM.

Boldface indicates illustrations.

PHOTO CREDITS

AD=Adobe Stock; AL=Alamy Stock Photo; DCP=Courtesy the Disney Consumer Products Creative Design team; DRMS=Dreamstime; GI=Getty Images; SS=Shutterstock; WDA=Courtesy of the Walt Disney Archives Photo Library; WDI=Walt Disney Imagineering

Cover, DCP; 1, DCP; 2, DCP; 3, DCP; 4-5, Molly Riley/Reuters; 5 (bursts), Kindlena/SS; 6 (UP), Michael Serraillier/Gamma-Rapho via GI; 6 (LO), solarseven/SS; 6 (wheels), Nykonchuk Oleksii/SS; 7 (UP), Ricardo Ramirez Buxeda/Orlando Sentinel via ZUMA Wire; 7 (LO), sripfoto/SS; 8-9 (all), WDA; 10 (LE), WDA; 10 (UP RT), Kent Phillips/Disney; 10 (LO RT), Peangdao/SS; 11, Sarah L. Gardner/NG Staff; 11 (flag), David Smart/SS; 12 (UP), Singleline/SS; 12 (lightning bolts), mhatzapa/SS; 12 (LO), Disney Enterprises/Photofest; 13 (UP LE), DCP; 13 (LO LE), Africa Studio/SS; 13 (RT), Edwin Verin/SS; 14-15 (background), Frederick Langrange/Disney; 14 (LE), Eric Isselée/AD; 14 (leaves), kvdkz/AD; 14 (RT), Olena/AD; 15, Richard Peterson/SS; 16 (LE), DCP; 16 (LO LE), rangizzz/SS; 16 (RT), WDA; 17 (UP LE & LO LE), KariHoglund/GI; 17 (UP CTR), Feng Yu/SS; 17 (UP RT), Li Ding/AD; 17 (LO RT), WDI Photography; 18, WDA; 19, Disney; 20, NASA/Johns Hopkins University Applied Physics Laboratory/Carnegie Institution of Washington; 21 (map), ink drop/AD; 21 (UP RT), Kent Phillips/Disney; 21 (LO), AaronP/Bauer-Griffin/GC Images/GI; 22 (UP LE), Coffeemill/SS; 22 (UP RT), Ilya Akinshin/SS; 22 (LO LE), Valentinar/DRMS; 22 (LO RT), Mikesilent/SS; 22 (stone), mrkevvzime/AD; 23 (UP LE), WDA; 23 (LO LE), peace_art/SS; 23 (UP CTR), Sarah L. Gardner/NG Staff; 23 (CTR LE), Preston Mack/Disney; 23 (CTR RT), Sarah L. Gardner/NG Staff; 23 (LO CTR), Sarah L. Gardner/NG Staff; 23 (LO RT), Sarah L. Gardner/NG Staff; 24 (UP), Soonthorn/AD; 24 (LO), Chloe Rice/Disney; 25, Everett Collection, Inc.; 26-27, Disney; 28 (LE), DCP; 28 (UP RT), Vibe Images/SS; 28 (hat), Kathrine Jensen/SS; 28 (LO RT), 32 pixels/AD; 29 (UP), StanislavBeloglazov/SS; 29 (LO), Walt Disney Pictures/Photofest; 30, RKO Radio Pictures/Photofest; 31 (LE), DCP; 31 (UP RT), Hayk_Shalunts/SS; 31 (LO RT), DCP; 32-33, WDA; 33 (UP), The Picture Art Collection/AL; 34-35 (stars), Allexxandar/SS; 34 (LO), Vector Tradition SM/SS; 35 (UP RT), DCP; 35 (LO), Kletr/AD; 36 (LE), Zadorozhnyi Vikto/SS; 36 (RT), DCP; 37, Art of Drawing/AL; 38, Wead/AD; 38 (pizza), Viktor/AD; 39 (UP), DCP; 39 (music), oleganko/SS; 39 (LO), MediaNews Group/Orange County Register via GI/Contributor; 40 (castle), Olga Thompson/Walt Disney World Resort via GI; 40 (scroll), Vadim Sadovski/SS; 40 (knight), topvectors/AD; 40 (LO), Douglas Carr/AL; 41 (LE), WDA; 41 (RT), Bob Desmond/Disney; 41 (hoop), sergiy1975/AD; 41 (ball), Africa Studio/SS; 42-43, DCP; 44 (UP LE), Gene Duncan/Disney; 44 (wind), John Takai/SS; 44 (RT), Eric Isselee/SS; 44 (LO LE), DCP; 45, VIAVAL/AL; 46 (UP), Walt Disney Pictures/Photofest; 46 (lion), Eric Isselee/SS; 46 (buffalo), Isselee/DRMS; 46 (boar), Eric Isselée/AD; 46 (gorilla), Eric Isselee/SS; 46 (wolf), Iakov Filimonov/SS; 46 (bear), vesta48/AD; 46 (LO), Pixel-Shot/AD; 47 (UP), Viavaltours/DRMS; 47 (clouds), Sealstep/SS; 47 (LO), WDI Photographer; 48 (LE), DCP; 48 (UP RT), WDA; 48 (LO RT), Disney; 49, WDA; 50-51, Disney; 52 (background), Nataliya Hora/DRMS; 52 (RT), Delphotostock/AD; 53 (LE), Boris Stroujko/SS; 53 (UP RT), WDI; 53 (LO RT), Nancy Nehring/GI; 54, jolly_photo/SS; 55, SMUKA/AL; 55 (LO LE), Itana/SS; 56-57, Kent Phillips/Disney; 58-59 (background), Natalia/AD; 58, Sarah L. Gardner/NG Staff; 59, CBS via GI; 60 (UP LE), Gerardo Mora/GI; 60 (UP CTR), Michael Thompson/DRMS; 60 (LO), NOAA Office of Ocean Exploration and Research, 2019 Southeastern U.S. Deep-sea Exploration; 61, DCP; 61 (UP LE), anaumenko/AD; 62 (grunge background), Miloje/SS; 62 (RT), DCP; 63, RSBPhoto1/AL; 63 (inset), Olga Danylenko/SS; 64, NG Maps; 65, Fred Prouser FP/Reuters; 65 (gold), Ron Dale/SS; 66 (UP), Lightfield Studios/AD; 66 (LO), DCP; 67, Ralph Alswang/William J. Clinton Presidential Library; 68 (confetti), Olga Rom/SS; 68 (candles), Srdjan Stefanovic/GI; 68 (LO LE), DCP; 68 (UP RT), onairjiw/AD; 68 (face), EkaterinaP/SS; 68 (LO RT), biancardi/SS; 69, WDA; 70, Vanessa Hunt/WDI; 71, Yuliia Davydenko/DRMS; 72 (LE), DCP; 72 (RT), MGM/Photofest; 73 (LE), Muzhik/SS; 73 (ornaments), graphixmania/SS; 73 (UP RT), Denis Belitsky/SS; 73 (pumpkin), topseller/SS; 73 (LO RT), Westhimal/DRMS; 74 (background), David Johnson/AD; 74 (bat), SP Vector Art/SS; 74 (tiger), apple2499/AD; 75, BigNazik/AD; 76 (LE), Disney; 76 (UP RT), dzmitry/AD; 76 (LO RT), paketesama/AD; 77 (LE), Trifonenko Ivan/AD; 77 (LO LE), WDA; 77 (RT), stokkete/AD; 77 (UP RT), WDA; 78-79, Lukas/AD; 78 (LO), WDA; 80 (LE), Inara Prusakova/SS; 80 (UP RT), LedyX/SS; 80 (LO RT), Ilya Akinshin/SS; 81 (UP), DCP; 81 (LO LE & LO RT), WDA; 82-83, Chris/AD; 84 (UP), DCP; 84 (LO), Mary Evans/Walt Disney Pictures/Pixar Animation Studios/Ronald Grant/Everett Collection, Inc.; 85, DCP; 86, DCP; 87 (UP), DCP; 87 (LO RT), Boris Rabtsevich/SS; 87 (Mickey), DCP; 88, WDI; 89 (LE), WDI; 89 (RT), Amineah/AD; 90 (UP), DCP; 90 (LO), Alexander Raths/AD; 91 (LE), DCP; 91 (UP RT), Chief Design/AD; 91 (LO RT), Silken Photography/SS; 92-93, DCP; 92, anatchant/AD; 93, DCP; 94, Mapics/AD; 94 (LO CTR), WDA; 95 (LE), Farinoza/AD; 95 (RT), DCP; 96 (LE), Prezoom/SS; 96 (UP RT), Antonio Gravante/SS; 96 (CTR RT), DCP; 97 (UP), Jess Allen/WDI; 97 (LO), WDI; 98 (LE), WDA; 98 (flames), rudvi/SS; 98 (UP RT), N Graphic/SS; 98 (LO RT), DCP; 99 (UP LE), NG Maps; 99 (notes), Pavel K/SS; 99 (LO LE), Bob Desmond/Disney; 99 (bubbles), hiro.y/AD; 99 (LO RT), Pineapple studio/AD; 100-101, Petr Salinger/SS; 100, DCP; 102 (all), WDI; 103, Matt Stroshane/Disney; 104 (UP LE), Fer Gregory/SS; 104 (LO LE), concept w/SS; 104 (RT), pukach/SS; 104 (air), Tori Art/AD; 104 (popcorn), Ilya Akinshin/SS; 105 (UP), WDA; 105 (LO LE), Elena Schweitzer/SS; 105 (LO RT), WDA; 106-107, WDA; 107, Tom/AD; 108 (LE), DCP; 108 (UP RT), WDI; 108 (LO RT), EcoView/AD; 109, OLC Photographer/WDI; 109 (UP RT), Ilya Akinshin/SS; 110, Hway Kiong Lim/SS; 111, Darryl Brooks/DRMS; 111 (Mickey), DCP; 112 (UP LE), faraktinov/AD; 112 (LO LE), University of Southern California/Corbis Historical/GI; 112 (UP RT), Kent Phillips/Walt Disney World Resort; 112 (LO RT), Kenishirotie/AD; 113, DCP; 114-115, Katie Roser/WDI; 114 (notes), trinurul/AD; 116, WDA; 117 (LE), Mike Pucher/WDI; 117 (UP RT), DCP; 117 (LO RT), WDI; 118 (LE), zxczxc80/AD; 118 (confetti), pixellebe/SS; 118 (TV), dreamerve/SS; 118 (static), Wakajawaka/SS; 118 (LO RT), vencav/AD; 118 (hat), DCP; 119 (LE), DCP; 119 (RT), Enrique/AD; 120, Walt Disney Studios Motion Pictures/Everett Collection, Inc.; 120 (UP LE), Milous Chab/DRMS; 121, Lucy Clark/AL; 122 (UP), bischy/GI; 122 (LO), Bernie Epstein/AL; 123 (UP LE), WDA; 123 (LO LE), Chloe Rice/Disney; 123 (RT), doomu/AD; 124 (LE), DCP; 124 (flags), twixx/AD; 124 (LO RT), Natalia Zakharova/DRMS; 125 (cassowary), Worakit Sirijinda/SS; 125 (ostrich), Gusak/AD; 125 (pheasant), RealityImages/AD; 125 (RT), DCP; 126 (LE), Danita Delimont/AD; 126 (UP RT), DCP; 126 (LO RT), NP27/SS; 127 (UP), DCP; 127 (LO), Courtesy Pixar; 127 (LO RT), Uros Petrovic/AD; 128, DCP; 129 (box), Mega Pixel/SS; 129 (slice), mhatzapa/SS; 130, Chloe Rice/Courtesy Disney; 131 (LE), NorthShoreSurfPhotos/AD; 131 (flag), Hugoht/DRMS; 131 (plate), Lonni/SS; 131 (UP RT), New Africa/AD; 131 (LO RT), amnaj/AD; 132-133, Laurent Viteur/GI; 133 (RT), DCP; 134 (LE), Kristyna Vagnerova/SS; 134 (bulb), crwpitman/SS; 134 (UP RT), kostikovanata/AD; 134 (LO RT), Tim UR/SS; 135, DCP; 136 (UP), Jess Allen/WDI; 136 (LO), Melica/SS; 137 (UP CTR), Disney; 137 (UP RT), Shino Iwamura/SS; 137 (LO), DCP; 138-139, Disney; 140, WDA; 141 (UP LE), Rasulov/SS; 141 (LO LE), Matthew Beard/Disney; 141 (UP RT), COLOA Studio/SS; 141 (LO RT), Jess Allen/WDI; 142 (UP), Walt Disney Studios Motion Pictures/Photofest; 142 (LO), DCP; 142 (gum), Madlen/SS; 143 (UP LE), NG Maps; 143 (UP CTR), Stuart Armstrong; 143 (license plate), TeddyandMia/AD; 143 (door), DCP; 143 (LO RT), DCP; 144-145, DCP; 144-145 (banner), Exposurestonature/DRMS; 146 (UP), DCP; 146 (LO), Richard/AD; 147, Alice Nerr/AD; 147 (CTR RT), Photofest/Buena Vista Pictures; 147 (clouds), Giraphics/SS; 148, Nicolas Larento/AD; 148 (CTR), gavran333/AD; 149 (UP LE), Srdjan Stefanovic/GI; 149 (LE), Courtesy Disney; 149 (UP RT), Stephen Shugerman/GI; 149 (LO RT), DCP; 150 (UP), DCP; 150 (snowflake), Kichigin/SS; 150 (LO), SerkanSenturk/AL; 151 (frost), XONOVETS/SS; 151 (UP LE), Dirk Van Geel/500px/GI; 151 (LO LE), DCP; 151 (UP RT), Timwege/DRMS; 151 (LO RT), Iakov Filimonov/SS; 152 (background), Maks Narodenko/AD; 152 (LE), Gubin Yury/SS; 152 (RT), Aaron Amat/SS; 153 (all), coffeemill/AD; 154 (UP), Kozkik/SS; 154 (LO), Andrea Barnett/Disney; 155, PolarPolar/SS; 155 (LO RT), Kent Phillips/Disney; 156-157, Ivan/AD; 158 (background), Morozova Oxana/SS; 158 (thread), Bunphot Kliaphuangphit/SS; 158 (silk), Khakimullin Aleksandr/SS; 158 (crystals), Julie Boro/AD; 159 (background), Coldmoon Photopro/SS; 159 (CTR), WDA; 160 (LE), WDI; 160 (UP RT), Sabina Schaaf/AD; 160 (brick), Dan Kosmayer/SS; 160 (LO RT), dule964/AD; 161, Andrea Barnett/Disney; 162, Jeff Nickel/Disney; 163 (UP), WDA; 163 (LO), Ratnakorn Piyasirisorost/GI; 164-165 (background), Creatus/AD; 164, Courtesy Pixar; 166 (LE), TAW4/AD; 166 (sticks), All For You/SS; 166 (RT), Isaac74/AL; 166 (CTR RT), Kent Phillips/Disney; 167 (background), Cattallina/AD; 167 (UP LE), Nathapol Kongseang/SS; 167 (UP RT), Mitch/AD; 167 (LO RT), serikbaib/AD; 168 (UP LE), DCP; 168 (CTR LE), anonpichit/AD; 168 (LO LE), iadams/AD; 168 (UP RT), Ilya Rumyantsev/AD; 168 (LO RT), gunungkawi/AD; 169 (UP), WDA; 169 (CTR LE), Steve Byland/DRMS; 169 (CTR RT), Paul Vinten/AD; 169 (LO), DCP; 170, SpicyTruffel/AD; 170 (CTR), Thomas/AD; 171, WDA; 172 (LE), DCP; 172 (CTR), Jennifer Read; 172 (RT), Talvi/SS; 173, Gerry Ellis/Photodisc; 173 (UP LE), 12bit/SS; 174 (UP), Disney; 174 (LO), Verock/SS; 175, NASA/JSC; 176, DCP; 176 (music), agrus/AD; 177, WDA; 178 (all), Courtesy Disney; 179 (UP LE), Kjpargeter/SS; 179 (LO LE), ProfiTrollka/AD; 179 (RT), Lysogor Roman/SS; 179 (UP RT), Comauthor/AD; 180, DCP; 181 (LE), nazarkru/AD; 181 (medal), aguiters/SS; 181 (UP CTR), NASA/JSC; 181 (RT), Disney; 182, DCP; 183, Courtesy Pixar; 184 (LE), Courtesy Pixar; 184 (UP RT), Superheang168/SS; 184 (LO RT), stable/SS; 185 (UP), michelaubryphoto/AD; 185 (LO), Lainhamer/DRMS; 186 (LE), WDA; 186 (UP RT), Courtesy of Solvang Bakery/Photography by Becky Hale/NG Staff; 186 (bees), vtupinamba/iStock Photo/GI; 186 (LO RT), NASA Goddard; 187, MediaPunch Inc/AL; 188, WDA; 188 (UP), warmworld/AD; 189 (LE), QQ7/AD; 189 (CTR LE), DCP; 189 (RT), donatas1205/SS; 189 (LO RT), DCP; 190-191, Jakl Lubos/SS; 192 (UP), albund/SS; 192 (stars), natakukushkina/AD; 192 (LO), Courtesy Pixar; 193 (LE), Twins Design Studio/AD; 193 (LO LE), Jakub Krechowicz/SS; 193 (RT), Supa Chan/SS; 193 (balloons), Kirill/AD; 194 (UP), WDA; 194 (CTR), Trybex/SS; 194 (LO), Mariah Wild/Courtesy Disney; 195 (UP RT), lovely pet/SS; 195 (spit), Olga Moonlight/SS; 195 (LO), Mike Pucher/WDI; 196, DCP; 196 (UP RT), AB Photography/AD; 197, Rich Carey/SS; 197 (lights), David Sandonato/DRMS; 197 (LO), DCP; 206, DCP

Since 1888, the National Geographic Society has
funded more than 14,000 research, conservation,
education, and storytelling projects around the
world. National Geographic Partners distributes
a portion of the funds it receives from your
purchase to National Geographic Society to support
programs including the conservation of animals and
their habitats. To learn more, visit natgeo.com/info.

For more information, visit nationalgeographic
.com, call 1-877-873-6846, or write to the following
address:

National Geographic Partners, LLC
1145 17th Street NW
Washington, DC 20036-4688 U.S.A.

For librarians and teachers: nationalgeographic
.com/books/librarians-and-educators

More for kids from National Geographic:
natgeokids.com

National Geographic Kids magazine inspires children
to explore their world with fun yet educational
articles on animals, science, nature, and more.
Using fresh storytelling and amazing photography,
Nat Geo Kids shows kids ages 6 to 14 the fascinating
truth about the world—and why they should care.
natgeo.com/subscribe

For rights or permissions inquiries, please contact
National Geographic Books Subsidiary Rights:
bookrights@natgeo.com

Designed by Eva Absher-Schantz

Trade paperback ISBN: 978-1-4263-7470-8
Reinforced library binding ISBN: 978-1-4263-7509-5

The publisher would like to thank the team that
made this book possible: Grace Hill Smith, editor;
Ariane Szu-Tu, editor; Sarah J. Mock, senior photo
editor; Alix Inchausti, senior production editor;
and Lauren Sciortino and David Marvin, associate
designers.

Printed in the United States of America
23/WOR/3 (PB)
23/WOR/2 (RLB)